Soccer Crazy

Sue Leather & Julian Thomlinson

D0584542

Series Editor: Rob Waring
Story Editor: Julian Thomlinson
Series Development Editor: Sue Leather

HEINLE
CENGAGE Learning™

Australia • Brazil • Japan • Korea • Mexico • Singapore • Spain • United Kingdom • United States

HEINLE
CENGAGE Learning

Page Turners Reading Library

Soccer Crazy

Sue Leather & Julian Thomlinson

Publisher: Andrew Robinson

Executive Editor: Sean Bermingham

Senior Development Editor:
Derek Mackrell

Assistant Editor: Sarah Tan

Director of Global Marketing:
Ian Martin

Content Project Manager:
Tan Jin Hock

Print Buyer:
Susan Spencer

Layout Design and Illustrations:
Redbean Design Pte Ltd

Cover Illustration: Eric Foenander

Photo Credits:
29 John Mena/Wikimedia Commons

ISBN-13: 978-1-4240-4653-9

ISBN-10: 1-4240-4653-X

Heinle
20 Channel Center Street
Boston, Massachusetts 02210
USA

Cengage Learning is a leading provider of customized learning solutions with office locations around the globe, including Singapore, the United Kingdom, Australia, Mexico, Brazil, and Japan. Locate your local office at:
international.cengage.com/region

Cengage Learning products are represented in Canada by Nelson Education, Ltd.

Visit Heinle online at **elt.heinle.com**

Visit our corporate website at
www.cengage.com

Printed in the United States of America
5 6 7 21 20 19 18 17

Contents

Background Reading

People in the story

Estela Ramos
Estela is captain of the
women's soccer team at
Brenton College. She wants
to play on the U.S. women's
team one day.

Katy Burns
Katy is Estela's friend. She
plays soccer on the women's
team. She's not very good
at soccer.

George Gray
George is the new coach of
the soccer teams at
Brenton College.

Professor Melanie Saunders
Professor Saunders is coach
of the taekwondo team at
Brenton College. She helps
students with their problems.

Mike Gomez
Mike is the captain of the
men's soccer team.

This story is set in Brenton, a college town in the
northwestern United States.

Chapter 1

Big news

"Estela!" calls Katy Burns.

Estela Ramos is running hard down the soccer field. She's tall and very pretty, with long dark hair. She runs very fast. Her friend, Katy, is running down the right side of the field. She has the ball at her feet. Katy's a young woman with blonde hair and a big smile.

"Katy, to me!" calls Estela. Katy kicks the ball to Estela, but it goes out.

"Oh, no! Sorry, Estela," Katy says.

"Let's try it again," says Estela. She smiles, but she thinks, *It's always like this.*

Estela's the captain of the women's soccer team at Brenton College. She loves the game and is really good. One day she wants to play for the U.S. women's team. But the other women on the team are not very good. Estela tries to help them. But it's not easy. Brenton doesn't usually win its college games. *We need some more good players,* thinks Estela. *We need more practice time. We need a good coach . . .*

"Hey, Estela," someone calls. "Come here."

It's Mike Gomez, the men's team captain.

"What does he want?" Katy asks. Estela looks at her watch. The women's practice finishes at five on Tuesdays. It's four-thirty now. The women can only have five hours practice a week. The men have ten. But they always want more.

"But it's not five o'clock," Estela calls. "You can wait!"

Mike walks over to them.

"It's not about that," he tells them. "There's some news. Big news."

His phone is in his hand. On it he's reading the college newspaper homepage, *thebrentonsun.com*.

Estela reads it out. "George Gray comes to Brenton." Then she says: "Oh, my . . . !"

"George Gray? Who's that?" asks Katy.

"An ex-England player!" says Mike.

Estela reads on. "George Gray comes to Brenton to coach our soccer teams," it says. "He played for England!"

"Is this good?" Katy asks.

"Good?" says Estela. "It's not just good. It's great!"

◇◇◇

One week later, Estela, Katy, and all the women's team are at soccer practice. Estela's very happy. It's the day George Gray starts as coach.

George Gray, Estela thinks. *With him as coach, we can be great. We can really play as a team. We can win our game against Martin College this Saturday. Then maybe can win the Championship!*

"He's not coming," says Katy.

"Yes, he is, Katy," she says. "He must come. He's here at the college, we know that!" *Where is he?* Estela thinks as she looks back toward the locker rooms. *It's four o'clock!*

"Let's start," she says to the women, and starts to run fast around the field. The women follow her, but they don't run fast.

Now it's five minutes after four, then ten minutes after four. George Gray isn't there.

"Well, he's a big name," says Katy. "A soccer star . . ."

"And so . . . ?"

"Maybe he doesn't want to coach a *women's* college team!" says Katy.

"Be quiet, Katy." Estela's getting angry. "You don't know that. Come on, let's practice."

The young women practice for forty-five minutes. Then they do some exercises. Then Estela puts them on two teams, and they play a short game. At five o'clock, the men are starting to come for their practice. Estela stops playing and looks at the men walking onto the field.

A tall man is with them. "That's George Gray!" Estela says.

George Gray runs onto the field with the men's team.

Gray is about 40 years old. He's wearing a blue tracksuit. Gray doesn't see the women. "Come on," he calls to the men. "I want to see you play!" The men start to play.

Estela watches Gray and the men for a minute. Gray is very good. He smiles a lot and runs up and down the field with them. He's helping them a lot. Soon they are playing very well. But Estela isn't happy. "This is very bad!" she says. "He's our coach too! Why doesn't he coach us?"

But the women don't say anything to Estela; they want to go now. "Come on, Estela," says Jacki, the goalkeeper. "We're going to Ben's Café." They start walking to the locker room. Estela goes with her friends. She has a good time, but later that night when she goes to bed, she can't sleep. She's thinking about George Gray. *Why doesn't he come to the girls' practice? Why doesn't he coach them?*

Chapter 2

A man's game?

The next day Estela gets up and goes to the college teachers' room. She asks to see George Gray. *Maybe he doesn't know about the women's soccer team,* she thinks.

George Gray comes to the door of the teachers' room. "What is it?" he asks.

She tells him about her team.

"We're OK," she says. "Some of us are good. But we aren't very good as a team. We need a really good coach. Someone like you."

George Gray listens for a minute. Then he says, "Women's soccer, you say? Do women really play soccer here?"

"Yes, Mr. Gray," says Estela. "They do." Estela knows that in England women don't often play soccer.

"Mmm," says Gray. "Well, the men need a lot of my time. They're good, but I want to coach them to win the Championship. I don't think I have time for the women, too . . ."

"Please, Mr. Gray," says Estela.

He looks at her. "Well, maybe on Thursday," he says.

"Thanks, Mr. Gray. I really want to show you what we can do." She walks away smiling.

On Thursday, George Gray comes to see the women practice. "Show me what you can do," he says to Estela and the other women on the team.

"OK." Estela's happy. *George Gray wants to help us,* she thinks. She puts the women on two teams, and they start to play. Estela's good, as always. She runs very fast and scores two goals.

After her second goal, Estela looks at George Gray. He's talking to one of the men from the men's soccer team. He isn't watching the women at all! He doesn't help them or say anything to them.

After the game, Estela's angry. "What do you think?" she asks Gray.

"About what?" asks Gray.

"About what?! About our team, that's what."

"Oh, very good," Gray says. He looks at his watch.

"What do we need to work on, then?" asks Estela.

"Listen, I need to talk to the men now. Let's talk later," Gray replies.

Gray walks away. Estela watches him. Her face goes red.

"Why don't you help us? Is it because you think soccer is a man's game?" she calls after him. "Is that it?"

Gray looks at her and smiles.

"A man's game," he says and thinks about it. "Yes, Estela. That's right."

Estela's angry, but she doesn't say anything to George Gray. She walks to the locker rooms. All her team is there. They're laughing and talking, but Estela doesn't talk or laugh. She's thinking about Gray. She's thinking about what she can do. She gets dressed and opens the door of the locker room.

"Where are you going?" asks Katy.

"I'm going to see Professor Saunders," says Estela. Professor Saunders is a teacher. She's Head of Media Studies at Brenton College. She's the coach of the taekwondo team, too. Saunders is sometimes tough, but she's a nice woman. *Maybe she can help,* thinks Estela.

Estela walks back to the college. It's a long walk, but she needs to think, and she needs to walk.

Twenty minutes later, Estela is outside Professor Saunders' room. Professor Saunders is coming out of her room. She is going to taekwondo practice and she's wearing a big red tracksuit.

Saunders looks at Estela. "Yes? What is it?"

Estela walks with the professor. The professor is a big woman who walks very fast. Estela tells her about George Gray. ". . . he's only coaching the men, and we need a coach too, Professor Saunders."

Melanie Saunders stops and looks at Estela. "But the man's new!" she says. "Give him time, Estela, give him time!"

"But . . ."

"Anyway," says Professor Saunders. "Please speak to Mr. De Veer. Not me."

De Veer, thinks Estela. *The vice-president of the college.* She knows that De Veer is not interested in the women's soccer team.

"I can't talk now," says Professor Saunders. "My taekwondo students are waiting for me." And with that, Professor Saunders walks away very fast.

Estela watches her go.

Now what? she thinks.

Chapter 3

The new coach

The next day, Estela meets Katy and the other women at Ben's Café.

"Professor Saunders says Mr. De Veer must do it," says Estela.

"De Veer . . . ? But he isn't interested . . ." Katy starts.

"I know, I know," says Estela. "I don't know who to talk to or what to do, Katy."

They don't talk for some minutes. They eat their sandwiches and have their cold drinks. Then Estela gets up to go.

"See you at soccer practice later . . ." Estela says.

"I don't know about practice . . . ," says Katy. "Some of the girls want to go to the movies. There's a new movie out . . ."

"What?" Estela looks at Katy. She isn't smiling. "Katy, you must come to practice. I'm the captain of this team and I'm telling you that you must come."

"But . . ."

"What, Katy?"

"Well, Gray doesn't think we're any good . . ."

Estela sits down again and looks at Katy. "Listen," she says, "you are good. We're good. We need a coach, that's all. Then we can be really good."

Katy smiles at Estela. "Maybe you're right," she says.

I am right, thinks Estela. *I must show everybody that this team is good. Maybe I can coach the team myself?*

Estela gets to soccer practice at about 3:30. She wants to practice alone for fifteen minutes before the other women come. She wants to think about how to coach them, too. *We must work as a team,* she thinks.

She goes to the locker room and sees George Gray outside the room. He's putting a piece of paper on the wall. "New Training Times" it says. "Your training time is later now," he says.

"What?"

"It's the evenings now," says Gray. "I need the afternoons for the men. They have the Championship next month."

Estela looks at the paper on the wall. She looks for the women's training times. Then she sees it. "Seven o'clock!!" she says. "You can't . . . That's . . . Nobody wants to come at that time!"

"It's OK," he says. "There are lights . . ."

"Then the men can have that time!" she says. Her face is red. She knows the women don't want to practice in the evening. There's dinner, and movies, and a lot of things to do!

"That's the only time there is," says Gray.

Estela is very angry. "You can't do this!" she says.

"I can do anything I like," says Gray.

"But . . . !"

"Miss Ramos," he says, "I'm the soccer coach at this college, and I'm telling you that your new training time is here!!" Gray gives her the paper.

They don't speak for some time.

"OK," says Estela, after a few minutes. "You don't like the women's soccer team, Mr. Gray, do you?"

George Gray doesn't reply.

Estela looks at him. "OK, Mr. Gray," she says. "I have an idea."

Gray looks at Estela.

"We play your men's team in a game," she goes on. "We win, you coach us. We don't win, we stop playing soccer here!"

"Win?" Gray laughs. "Play the men?"

"The men," says Estela.

"OK. Women against men!" He laughs. "You're crazy, Miss Ramos."

Crazy, am I? Estela thinks. *Let's see . . .*

Chapter 4

Soccer crazy

"You're crazy!" says Jacki, the goalkeeper. "Play the men?"

"We must do it!" says Estela. Her soccer team is at Ben's Café. They are talking about Gray and the game.

"But why?" some of the women on the team ask Estela.

"Because we must," says Estela. "We must show George Gray that we're good."

"Estela's right," says Katy. "We must be strong now. Or, we can't play soccer as a team at all."

The team talks for a long time. Then Estela says, "OK, no more talk. Now we must practice hard!"

"But . . ."

"Listen," says Estela. "You must help me. For the next weeks, we need to practice every day for two hours."

"Two hours!" some of the women say.

"It's the only way," says Estela.

The women talk more. "OK," they say, "we're with you, Estela."

◇◇◇

The game is the next week on Wednesday afternoon. For the next seven days, Estela and her team practice for two hours every day. They practice early in the morning and they practice late at night. They don't want the men's team to see them. They don't want George Gray to see them.

Estela makes them do exercises for the first hour. "Come on," she says, "The men are very fast and you're too slow!" The women work very hard, running with the ball and doing a lot of different exercises. They need to become strong and fast. Then, after the exercises, they play a game.

As always, Estela plays really hard. She takes the ball away from other players and scores a lot of goals. But the other women don't play well. They look tired and unhappy.

"Come on!" Estela calls. "We have the game next week. What's wrong with you?"

At first, nobody replies.

Then Katy says, "It's you, Estela."

"It's me? What do you mean, it's me?"

"You're really good at soccer. You always get the ball, you always score the goals."

"And?" Estela asks. "Is that bad?"

"It's not bad," Katy says. "But it's not really a team."

"What is it, then?" Estela says.

"You never give the ball to us. You always take it! That's not a team. Not really."

Everyone is quiet. Estela wants to say something, but doesn't. She knows Katy is right.

"You're right," she says. "OK, let's try again. This time, I'm not playing."

Estela sits down and watches the women play. She talks to them from the side of the field and tells them what to do.

"Run with the ball, Katy," she calls. "That's it. Now, kick it to Ying-Chu. Good, good!"

After the game, the women are happy.

"Thanks for that, Estela," they say.

"No, thank you," says Estela.

The last practice before the game, Estela plays with the team again. But she doesn't keep the ball to herself. She gives it to the other players, too. Everyone plays well, not only Estela. As they go back to the locker rooms, Estela looks at them. She feels proud. *We are good now,* she thinks. *But can we win?*

Chapter 5

A woman's game?

On Wednesday afternoon at two o'clock, Estela, Katy, and all the women's team go to the soccer field. They do some exercises to get ready for the game. The game starts at three o'clock. A few minutes before three o'clock, the men's team and George Gray are there.

"Come on, boys," says George Gray, as they walk onto the soccer field. Some of the men are smiling and laughing. They think a game against the women is easy. "OK, boys," says Mike Gomez, "5-0, I think."

Estela looks at Gomez but she doesn't say anything. *Let's see,* she thinks.

George Gray starts the game.

The men are slow to start. They think a game against women is easy. But the women run fast and play hard. Estela is everywhere, running, getting the ball. Mike Gomez tries to run with Estela, but he can't. She's very fast. "Come on, Mike," his friends call. "She's good!"

After about fifteen minutes, the women get a corner kick. Katy takes the ball. She kicks it to Estela in the center of the field. Mike Gomez tries to get the ball, but Estela is too fast. Estela takes the ball on her right foot and shoots toward the goal. The ball goes very fast

past the men's goalkeeper. All the women call out "Goal!" and run to Estela.

"That's not a goal," calls the captain. "It's offside!"

The women's team all look at George Gray. Gray says, "It isn't offside. It's a goal!" Then he calls out, "1-0." George Gray looks at the men. He's angry. "Come on, men!" he says.

Now the men start to play well. They run fast and get near the goal often. Jacki, the goalkeeper, needs to work very hard. She stops two or three goals, but a minute before half-time, the men score a goal. At half-time the score is 1-1.

"OK," says Estela to the women, as they drink juice and eat oranges. "That's good. But now we must work *really* hard."

In the second half, the game gets very difficult. One of the men kicks Julie Dokic very hard. Estela walks across the field to Julie. "Come on," she says. She gives her hand to Julie. "Don't worry about him. He's angry because we're good."

George Gray gives the boy a yellow card. But after an hour of the game, the men score again. One player runs past the women's defenders and scores a very good goal. It's 2-1 to the men, and the women are very tired.

"Come on!" calls Estela to the women. "The game isn't over." Then she gets the ball and runs a long way down the field with it. She gets past one, two, three men. She can score a goal, she thinks. But maybe it's good to pass the ball to Katy. "It's yours, Katy," she calls. Then she kicks the ball very hard to Katy. "Come on, Katy, score!" she calls. Katy takes it and kicks the ball hard. It goes past the goalkeeper and into the goal. "2-2!" calls George Gray. "Good goal, Katy," all the women call. Katy looks very happy.

There are only a few minutes to play. The men play hard, the women play hard. The men try to score a goal. The women try to stop the men, but in the last minute of the game, the men score a goal. It's 3-2! George Gray looks at his watch. It's time. The ninety minutes are over. He stops the game.

Estela and the women walk off the soccer field. "Good game!" all the women say to Estela. "You're great!"

"Thank you," she says to them. "You're great, too! I'm really proud of you." Estela smiles, but her face is sad. "Thanks, Estela," says Katy. "Giving me the ball . . . We're a good team now!"

"No," says Estela. "It's because of all of us."

The women go to the locker room, but Estela sits down on the field. She puts her head in her hands. She sits there for a long time.

◇◇◇

"Estela?"

Estela looks up. It's George Gray.

"You look sad," says Gray.

"I *am* sad," says Estela.

"Why?"

"Because that's it!" says Estela.

"What?" asks Gray.

"No more women's soccer team," says Estela. She doesn't look at Gray. She looks down. "And what about me? I want to play soccer for the U.S. team one day. How can I do that now?"

"You're very good," says Gray.

Estela looks up.

"Very, very good," he says. "Your team's great, too!"

"Do you really think we're great?" asks Estela.

"Yes, I do," says George Gray. "I'm sorry, Estela," he goes on. "I'm very sorry. Before, I . . ."

Estela looks at George Gray. *Is he really saying that she's good? Is he really saying that her team's good?*

"From now on, I want to work with you," he says. "Can I be your coach?" He's smiling.

"Really?" says Estela. She gets up. "You want to coach us?" She's smiling, too.

"Yes, really!" says George Gray.

Estela thinks for a minute. Then she says, "Can we have ten hours practice, like the men?"

"Yes, you can," George Gray says. He's laughing now. "After all, soccer is a woman's game, too."

Review

A. Match the characters in the story to their descriptions.

1. _____ Mr. De Veer   **a.** a famous soccer player from England
2. _____ Estela Ramos   **b.** the captain of the men's team
3. _____ George Gray   **c.** the captain of the women's team
4. _____ Melanie Saunders   **d.** the coach of the taekwondo team
5. _____ Mike Gomez   **e.** the vice-president of Brenton College

B. Complete the summary using the sentence endings in the box.

> **a.** think it is easy to beat the women
> **b.** play against the men's team
> **c.** asks if he can be their coach
> **d.** stop playing soccer here
> **e.** think soccer is a man's game
> **f.** practice hard everyday for two hours

Estela Ramos is very excited—George Gray, a famous soccer player, is coming to Brenton College! She hopes that he can help the women's team play better. But Gray does not want to train the girls. No one, not even Professor Saunders, wants to help them. This is because many people **1.** _____ . Estela has an idea—the women's team will **2.** _____ . "We win, you coach us. We don't win, we **3.** _____ ," she tells Coach Gray. The game is in one week's time and the girls **4.** _____ . Estela learns to pass the ball to her teammates. During the match, the girls play very well. The boys are surprised because they **5.** _____ . Both sides play hard and the boys beat the girls 3-2. But Estela is happy because Coach Gray **6.** _____ . He finally sees that soccer is a woman's game, too.

C. Complete this crossword.

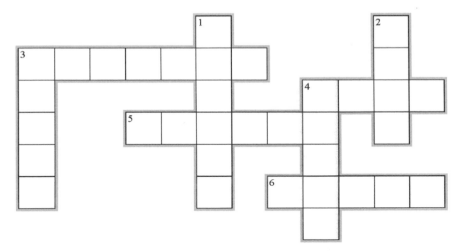

Across

3. The leader of a sports team is called the _____ .

4. There are 11 players on a soccer _____ .

5. The goal _____ stops the ball from going into the net.

6. Soccer players play in an area called a _____ .

Down

1. A soccer game lasts _____ minutes.

2. You get one point if you score a _____ .

3. A _____ is someone who trains a sports team.

4. A team must _____ hard if they want to get better.

Background Reading:
Spotlight on ... *Women's Soccer*

Soccer is often seen as a man's game, but women's soccer has a long history. Today, it is more popular than ever. In the USA, women's soccer is even more popular than men's.

Late 19th century	1921	1951	1991	1996
Women start playing soccer for exercise and fun.	The English Football Association bans women's soccer competitions.	The first organized women's league in USA is set up.	The first women's World Cup is played in China. USA wins.	Women's soccer becomes an Olympic sport.

Mia Hamm: Soccer Star

Full name	Mariel Margaret Hamm
Date of birth	March 17, 1972
Place of birth	Selma, Alabama, United States
Height	5 ft 5 in (1.65 m)
Playing position	Forward

Top 10 Women's Soccer Teams

1. USA
2. Germany
3. Brazil
4. Sweden
5. North Korea
6. Japan
7. Norway
8. England
9. France
10. Denmark

Source: FIFA rankings, December 2009

U.S. player Mia Hamm is the best-known women's soccer player of all time. She has scored more international goals than any other man or woman in history—158 goals in 275 games. She played her last game in 2004, soon after helping the U.S. team win at the Olympic Games in Athens. Hamm is also the author of *Go for the Goal: A Champion's Guide to Winning in Soccer and Life.*

Think About It

1. Do you know of any famous female sports stars?
2. Do you think women's soccer will be as popular as men's soccer one day?

Glossary

captain	(*n.*)	the leader of a sports team
championship	(*n.*)	a sports competition where several teams try to win
coach	(*n.*)	the manager of a sports team who helps the team
exercise(s)	(*n.*)	movement of your body to practice a sport
(soccer) field	(*n.*)	the place people play soccer
goal	(*n.*)	the place you try to kick the ball when playing soccer
(score a) goal	(*v.*)	to put the soccer ball in the goal
locker room	(*n.*)	the place people change clothes to play sports
media studies	(*n.*)	studies about TV, radio, newspapers, and so on
offside	(*adj.*)	breaking the rules by being too near the goal when playing soccer
practice	(*v.*)	to do something again and again so you get good at it
proud	(*adj.*)	feeling good because you did something well
taekwondo	(*n.*)	a Korean sport
team	(*n.*)	a group of players who play a sport together
tough	(*adj.*)	hard, difficult
tracksuit	(*n.*)	sports clothes
vice-president	(*n.*)	a very important person at a university
win	(*v.*)	to get more points than the other team